# WHY WE RAGE

## THE SCIENCE OF ANGER

by Melissa Mayer

Consultant:
**Eric H. Chudler, Ph.D.**
Research Associate Professor
Department of Bioengineering
University of Washington
Seattle, WA

COMPASS POINT BOOKS
a capstone imprint

Compass Point Books are published by Capstone,
1710 Roe Crest Drive, North Mankato, Minnesota 56003
www.capstonepub.com



**Editorial Credits**
Gina Kammer, editor, Kellie M. Hultgren, editor; Brann Garvey, designer; Tracy Cummins, media researcher; Tori Abraham, production specialist

**Photo Credits**
iStockphoto: kate_sept2004, 42, SolStock, 49; Science Source: DR P. MARAZZI, 52, Science Picture Co, 51; Shutterstock: Africa Studio, 47, Alla Iatsun, 26, Antonio Guillem, 17, Bikeworldtravel, 28-29, Blamb, 14, Carlos Caetano, 5, Daisy Daisy, 30, Designua, 18, fizkes, 41, Gagliardi Photography, 33, Hayk_Shalunts, 57, juliawhite, 24, Master1305, Cover, Microgen, 37, odrakon, 21, Orange Vectors, 13, Rawpixel.com, 27, Sayan Puangkham, 23, Top Photo Engineer, 7, Valentyna Chukhlyebova, 25, Veres Production, 10

**Library of Congress Cataloging-in-Publication Data**
Names: Mayer, Melissa, author.
Title: Why we rage : the science of anger / by Melissa Mayer.
Description: North Mankato, Minnesota : Compass Point Books, [2020] | Series: Decoding the mind
Identifiers: LCCN 2019004144| ISBN 9780756562168 (hardcover) | ISBN 9780756562243 (pbk.) | ISBN 9780756562175 (ebook pdf)
Subjects: LCSH: Anger--Juvenile literature. | Anger--Physiological aspects--Juvenile literature. | Emotions--Juvenile literature.
Classification: LCC BF575.A5 M34 2020 | DDC 152.4/7--dc23
LC record available at https://lccn.loc.gov/2019004144

All internet sites appearing in back matter were available and accurate when this book was sent to press.

Printed in the United States of America.
PA71

# Table of Contents

CHAPTER 1

# Release the Rage Beast!

FROM THE MOMENT you walk into your room, something feels off. Then you see it. Your journal—with your most private thoughts—isn't where you left it. You feel your face flush with anger. Your jaw clenches, and prickly heat runs down your arms to your balled-up fists. Without thinking, you lash out and sink that fist deep into the drywall.

If you are human, you have no doubt felt anger. Everyone does at some point—and the feeling that your anger is sometimes out of control may be more common than you think. If you've ever felt as though a rage beast lives inside you, understanding the science behind that anger can help you take back control. A big part of staying in control is finding the right balance for your reactions. While it isn't good for you to hold in anger, it's not healthy for you to rage, either.

# Inside the Rage Cage

Anger is a strong feeling of displeasure (even to the point of wanting to hurt someone) that arises when we feel we have been treated badly. The last part matters a lot. Anger is a normal human response to something that feels like a violation. We feel anger about a lot of things. Many are personal, like getting a bad grade or tripping over the shoes that your brother promised to put away. Others are much bigger than one person, such as when one group of people steps all over the rights of another group. Rage is anger that is uncontrolled, intense, and even violent.

One common reason for anger is not getting the things you need to survive. According to psychologist Mitch Abblett, during the years between middle school and adulthood, most people have four core needs, outside of the obvious survival stuff. Growing up, you, like most people, do best when you have the following:

- **Respect from people around you**. You are probably pretty good at handling your life already. It makes sense to want people to see that and treat you like the capable person you are.
- **Space to figure out life on your own terms.** The room you need to grow is probably both physical and emotional. It's hard to explore life and your own identity with someone breathing down your neck.
- **Validation of your feelings.** Growing up is intense. It helps when the people you care about make it clear that the things you feel are real and that they matter.
- **Peers who make you feel that you belong.** You want to feel like you fit in with a group of friends. Being accepted often requires having the right clothes, devices, or access to entertainment (or money to buy them), so this core need also includes the stuff required to fit in.

The things you want—and the reasons you might feel angry—aren't limited to not having those core needs met. But if you feel the rage beast inside you start to rattle its cage, checking for violations in those areas is a good place to start figuring out why you're so angry.

You could probably guess that anger isn't a new thing. One of the first written descriptions of anger is from 320 BC—more than 2,300 years ago. At that time, the Greek philosopher Aristotle said anger is "a belief that we, or our friends, have been unfairly slighted, which causes in us both painful feelings and a desire or impulse for revenge." Not too far off, huh?

Anger is so important for humans that you probably started showing the emotion when you were only 2 months old. That's before you could even sit up and about the time you gave the world your first real smile.

# Meet the Anger Disorders

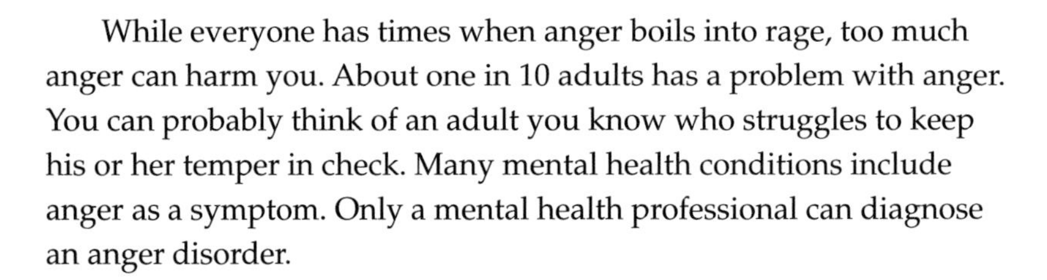

While everyone has times when anger boils into rage, too much anger can harm you. About one in 10 adults has a problem with anger. You can probably think of an adult you know who struggles to keep his or her temper in check. Many mental health conditions include anger as a symptom. Only a mental health professional can diagnose an anger disorder.

### Anxiety and depression

These are very common. Sometimes the main symptom isn't panic, worry, or sadness, as you might expect. Angry outbursts and irritability are signs of these conditions too. Sometimes anger acts as a mask to hide anxiety or depression.

### Post-traumatic stress disorder (PTSD)

This is a web of symptoms that appear after a terrifying event. PTSD can make you feel as if you are always on edge or ready to act out. Anger linked with PTSD may look like bursts of rage, irritability, or self-harm.

### Intermittent explosive disorder

This usually brings episodes of violence or aggression that seem to come out of nowhere. These episodes can be verbal or physical. They are out of proportion to what sets them off. Right before an outburst, you might feel tingly or panicky.

# About one in 10 adults has a problem with anger.

Intermittent explosive disorder may be more common than once thought, affecting about 8 percent of teens.

## Disruptive behavior disorders such as oppositional defiant disorder (ODD) and conduct disorder

ODD is a pattern of angry outbursts and refusing to follow rules. Conduct disorder is a pattern of not respecting other people or their things. It may include violent behaviors, such as destroying property or being cruel to people or animals.

## Personality disorders

The 10 identified personality disorders all affect how a person relates to other people and to the world. All of them involve long-term problems with unhealthy thought patterns, impulsive behavior, and trouble with expressing emotion. Some, such as antisocial personality disorder, borderline personality disorder, narcissistic personality disorder, and paranoid personality disorder, are linked to frequent feelings of anger.

## Adjustment disorder with disturbance of conduct

Adjustment disorders show up after a person experiences stressful change, such as major illness or the death of a close family member. People usually adjust within a few months of such a change, but sometimes the stress of the event remains fresh. When the disorder involves disturbance of conduct, symptoms include bursts of anger that may lead to fighting, vandalism, and other behaviors that break laws.

# Anger, the Ultimate Buzzkill

Hulking out into a rage can feel intense. But life as Bruce Banner, the mild-mannered scientist who morphs into the ultra-angry Hulk, is no picnic either. It's a heavy burden knowing your anger might burst out at any moment.

Out-of-control anger can make it hard to form and keep relationships. This means that you (or a friend) may have trouble managing your anger. You might take out your anger on other people, either by being aggressive or by sulking. This could make it difficult for other people to bond with you. You could feel alone at a time in your life when friendships, family ties, and other close relationships are especially important.

Stuffing down that anger hurts you too. Swallowing such a powerful emotion can make you feel bad about yourself. Holding in your anger can also make you anxious or depressed. And sometimes people use drugs or alcohol to escape from the way stuffed-down anger feels. Some experts say that addiction is a (dangerous) way of trying to comfort yourself after experiencing painful emotions.

When you're overwhelmed with rage, your body is dumping hormones into your blood to get you ready to deal with whatever has upset you. These hormones raise your heart rate and blood pressure. Over time, this can damage your cardiovascular system and increase the risk of stroke or heart attack. Stress hormones also lower your body's ability to fight off illness and to digest food properly, and they can even make your bones weaker. Sometimes feeling anger hurts in the moment too. Bursts of rage can bring headaches, including migraines, that feel terrible and make life difficult.

The word *anger* probably comes from the Old Norse word *angr*, which indicated grief and sorrow. Related words from the past include the Old German word *angust* (angst, anxiety) and the Latin word *angor* (anguish).

## IT'S A REAL RAGER

The news isn't all terrible! Some scientists think that people who tend to be angry are also more optimistic. It's as if the power of anger amps up the idea of what's possible. Researchers tested this using worst-case scenarios. When lots of people were in danger, angry people were more likely to try to rescue people. They were less likely to play it safe and more likely to be heroic.

The military knows this and uses it to build stronger soldiers. Special forces, such as the Navy SEALs, sometimes need to do things that require superhuman strength or stamina. To train for this, SEALs learn to harness surges of rage and use that energy to boost their performance.

Anger is a powerful tool for the average person too. It can be a signal that something is wrong. If you are in an unhealthy relationship of any kind, you might feel anger when the other person oversteps a boundary or does something else that's hurtful. That anger can help you negotiate for what you need or give you the strength to move on. It can do this for really big problems too. People who see social problems and want to fix them often rely on anger to power their work.

CHAPTER 2

# A Quick and Dirty Guide to Neuroanatomy

WHERE DOES ALL THAT RAGE COME FROM? To understand your anger, look no further than the real estate inside your head. Anger can affect your whole body, but your brain is where it starts.

## Meet Your Brain

You probably don't spend much time thinking about your sense of smell, but the candle industry sure does. Do you like horse sweat? Pizza? Fancy a bedroom that smells like the streets of New York? Or the Canadian prime minister? (Wait—what?) There's a candle for that.

Things you smell can change your mood and bring buried memories to the surface. Some smells make you feel as though you have fallen through a time warp. It's as if you are reexperiencing something pleasant or disgusting from your past.

It's easy to link smells with feelings because of the connections your brain builds between the areas that process your memories and emotions—your limbic system—and the areas associated with smell. These connections are so automatic that stores sometimes pump scents into the air to make you feel more relaxed or happy.

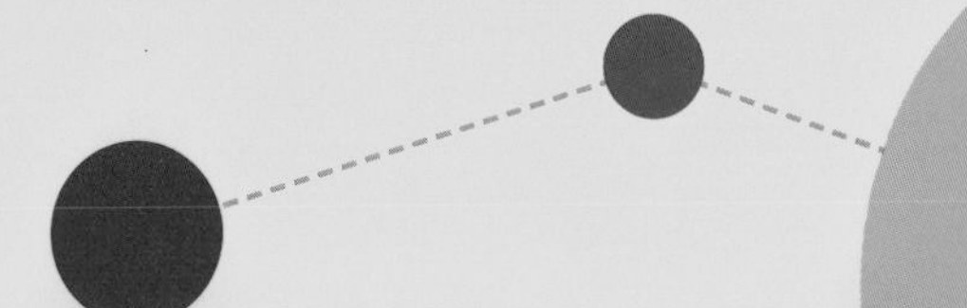

Your limbic system plays a role in emotional regulation. This is your ability to feel all of your emotions in an appropriate and flexible way. It means you can have spontaneous feelings yet also control your reactions. Ever wonder why adults don't (usually) throw tantrums like toddlers? That's emotional regulation at work. This system helps you feel and manage your anger.

Some of the key players in feeding the rage beast are the amygdala, hypothalamus, hippocampus, and prefrontal cortex. You don't need an advanced degree to get a handle on some of the roles played by these parts of your brain.

# Rage Feeders

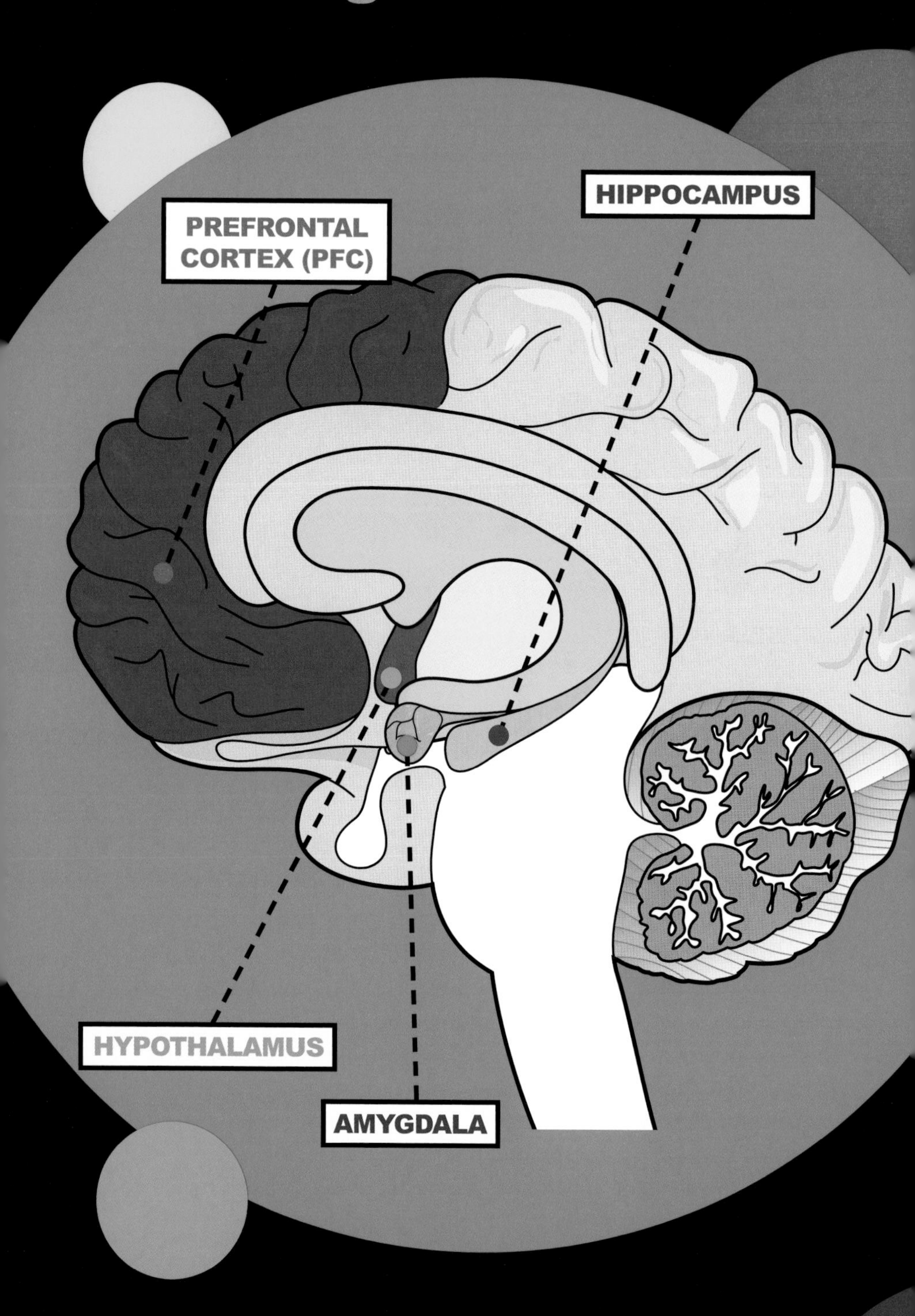

- **AMYGDALA:** Think of your amygdala as your brain's safety monitor. Its job is to take in data from your senses and pull the alarm as soon as it suspects danger. You get up in the night to get a drink and glimpse a figure lurking in the shadows. You throw your hands up to shove it away before you even think—and knock down the clothes you hung up to wear tomorrow. The danger signal that prompted you to act was brought to you by your amygdala.
- **HYPOTHALAMUS:** Your hypothalamus responds to the amygdala's alarm by sending chemical messages through your body. The messages make sure that every part of you is ready to respond to the threat together. This is why your hands reach up to fight off an intruder so quickly. Your body is working automatically as a unit.
- **HIPPOCAMPUS:** Your hippocampus helps to store your memories and assists the other parts of the limbic system with emotional regulation. Next time, you might remember that you put your clothes there, even if you're still half asleep.
- **PREFRONTAL CORTEX (PFC):** Your prefrontal cortex is the part of your brain that checks the big picture. Your PFC processes sensory data more slowly than your amygdala. It uses your memories and the extra information it gathers to consider all your options. After your amygdala sounds the alarm about the intruder in your room and you shove the danger away, your PFC points out the fact that the invader isn't moving—and looks kind of flat. It is your PFC that tells you the threat is not real. You don't have to fight off your clean laundry after all. Your PFC is part of your cortex, which is the big mass of wrinkly tissue you probably picture when you hear the word *brain*.

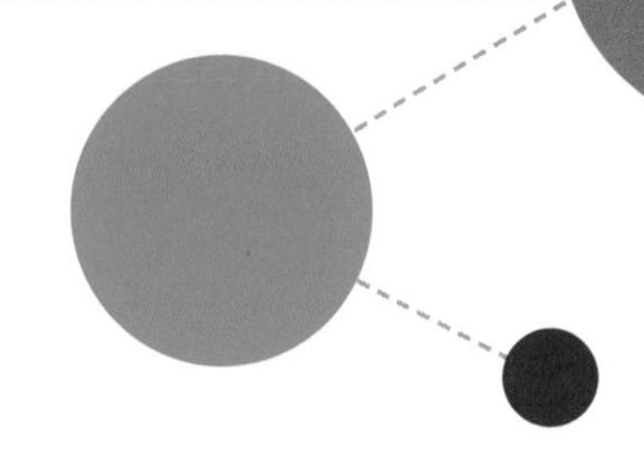

# Your Brain Talks to Itself

The various parts of your brain don't work alone, and they don't always agree with each other. To get your anger really going (and to stop it), all those areas of your brain need to communicate with each other. Navy SEALs and other members of the military may wear special helmets with transmitters so they can send messages back and forth during a mission. Your brain does this too. It uses chemicals called neurotransmitters that carry messages from nerve cell to nerve cell.

# Common Neurotransmitters and Possible Results

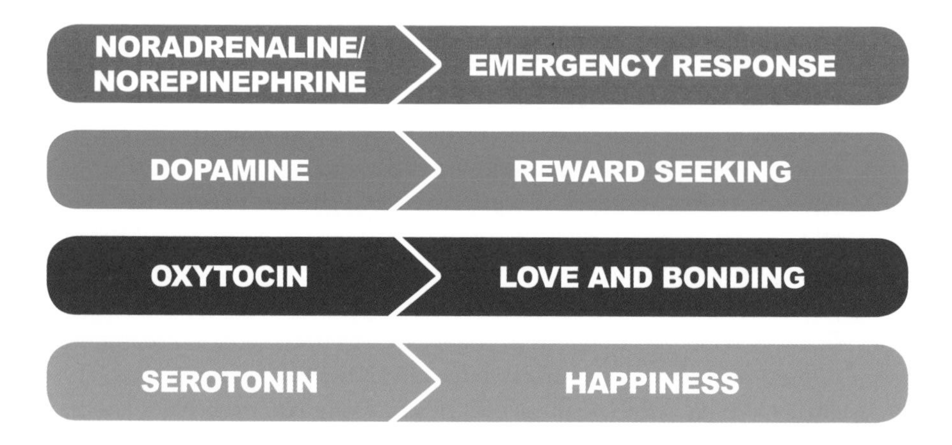

Picture this. You are arguing with your best friend when things take a bad turn. She brings up something private and uses it as a weapon to hurt you. While you are reeling from this betrayal, your friend gets right up in your face. Neither of you has ever been this mad. The air between you is almost crackling with intensity.

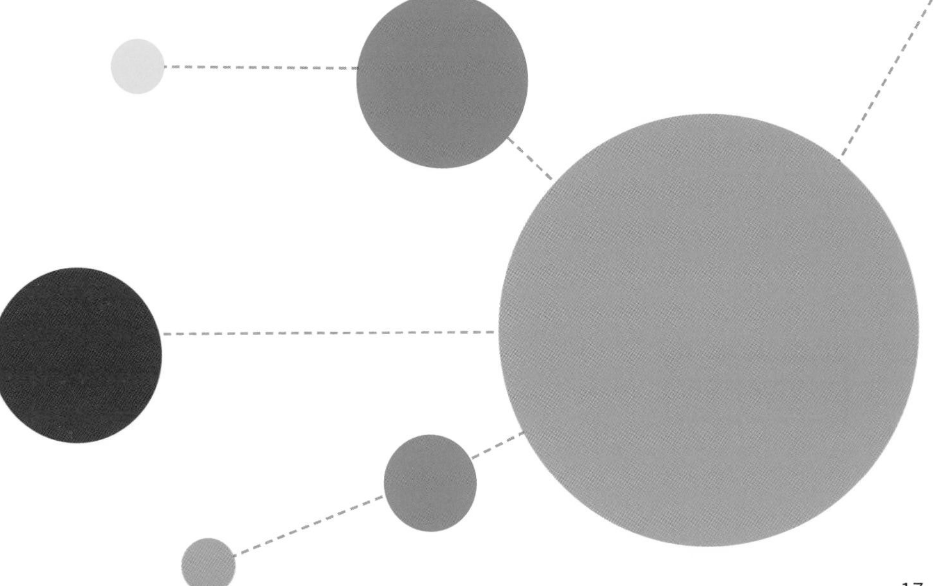

# A Neuron

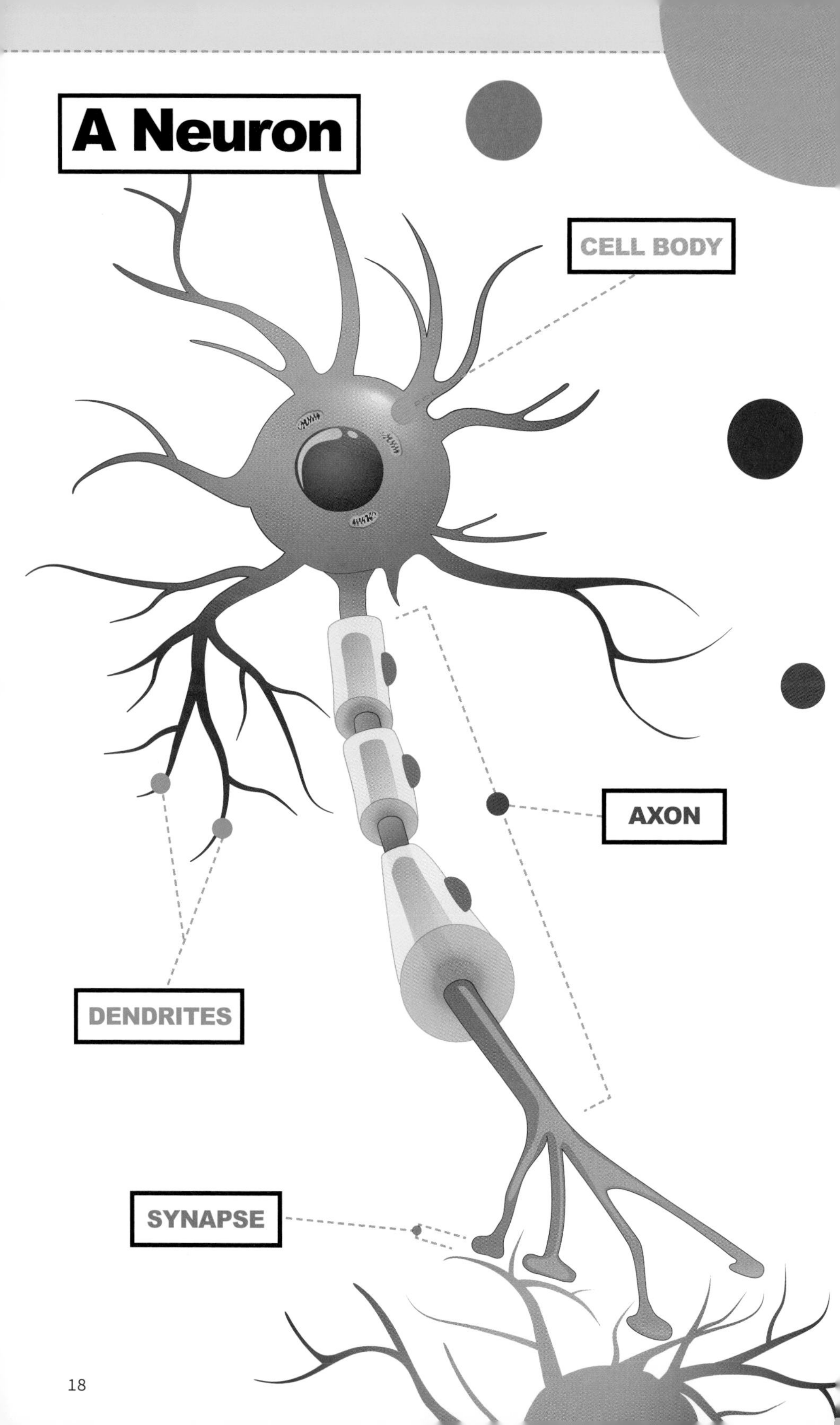

# Ready, Set, Rage!

Your friend screams at you. Inside your skull, your brain's nerve cells—neurons—fire rapidly. An electric signal runs down the long, tail-like axon of each neuron, launching neurotransmitters such as noradrenaline out of the end of the neuron. These chemical messages (Danger! Get ready to fight!) jump over the spaces between the neurons—the synapses—and are caught by the branchy arms of neighboring neurons.

As you stand there, about to slug your best friend, your neurons are doing what scientists call *firing together.* This means that when your neurons pass messages, their connection becomes stronger. The path the messages take from one nerve cell to the next becomes easier, and the messages move faster. Eventually, those pathways can become automatic. This is especially useful if you are learning to read or trying to get through a hard level in a video game. When neurons fire together over and over as you repeat a thought or task, the thing you're repeating becomes easier to do.

The way your neurons fire together also helps your brain understand the world. Neurons that fire together form circuits and create associations in your mind. This is why you might react to a practical joke with laughter or rage, depending on your history with pranks. It's also why one person can see a snake and have cuddly thoughts while someone else feels fear.

"Cells that fire together wire together."

***Carla Shatz,*** PhD, neurobiologist and first woman to head the department of neurobiology at Harvard University

# Your Rage Circuit

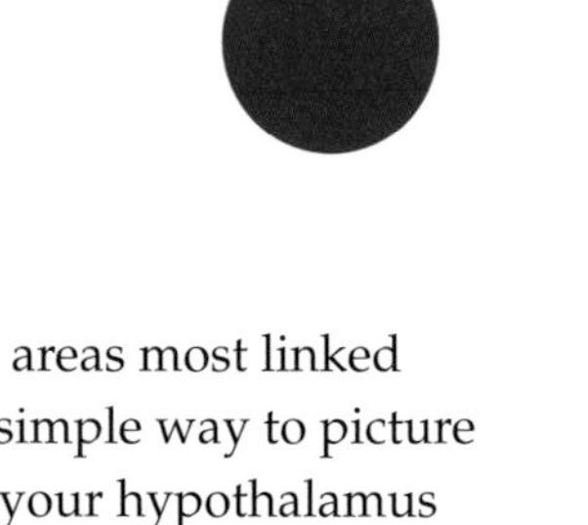

R. Douglas Fields, a neuroscientist, calls the areas most linked with anger and aggression the *rage circuit*. It's a simple way to picture a complex idea. The chemical messages sent by your hypothalamus trigger automatic responses in your body. That's why you don't have to tell your heart to beat faster when a bigger person threatens you. Your hypothalamic attack region has that covered. This small cluster of neurons is closely tied to the rage response. In fact, when scientists give this area in a mouse's brain a small shock, the animal will instantly attack its cage mate. According to Fields, that's because this part of the brain controls the urge to fight back when threatened.

If you play a video game several times a week, it gets easier to remember the key combinations for blasting enemies. In the same way, triggering the neural pathways associated with rage over and over makes them easy to use. This means that if you deal often with stress, trauma, or other circumstances that set off a rage response, your anger comes faster. It might even cause you to snap over small things. Think about that fight with your friend. You can react by shouting. Or you can take a breath and let the rage messages firing in your brain calm down first. When you do this, you are also teaching your brain how to handle conflict in the future.

**. . . if you deal often with stress, trauma, or other circumstances that set off a rage response, your anger comes faster.**

# EVEN YOUR GENES ARE MAD

Some people think having a quick temper is just part of who they are—like their eye color or height. Maybe you notice that other people in your family also get angry easily. Just as many physical traits run in families, so do mental health disorders. For example, having a close family member with anxiety or depression means it is more likely that you will become anxious or depressed.

However, the genetics of behavior is more complex than the color of your eyes. Even if your short fuse is just like that of one or both of your birth parents, it's still hard to figure out how much of that comes from your genes and how much comes from your environment. If you live with angry people, you might pick up those behaviors no matter what your DNA encodes.

Still, unraveling human genes is exciting. Scientists have found a few genes that might be tied to aggression and risk-taking. One of them, called the *warrior gene*, changes the messages carried by some neurotransmitters, including serotonin and dopamine. Another gene, which goes by the less memorable name *CDH13*, also affects messages between cells. These two genes have been linked with aggression, and they appear to be passed down. But experts point out that having a variant of one of these genes doesn't mean you will Hulk out. And people with such a variant who do act aggressively also have other risk factors for violence, such as early life abuse or addiction.

If you think you might have a quick temper—due to either your DNA or your environment—consider viewing it as a super power. At times that trait could help you and other people—just as it does the Special Forces. But that means you need to be extra careful about when and how you use anger. Remember the message of Spider-Man: "With great power there must also come—great responsibility!"

CHAPTER 3

# Fight or Flight (or Freeze):

## The Value of Courage

THE SUN SET SOONER THAN YOU EXPECTED, and the walk home is barely lit by widely spaced streetlights. As you step from a pool of light into the shadows, someone approaches you from behind and grabs your jacket. You feel a burst of rage. Without thinking, you whip around and shove the person as hard as you can. Before you even process what is happening, your fist connects with a face.

Or maybe you shrug out of your coat and make a break for it. You run as fast and far as you can without looking back. Or—worst case—your body betrays you. You desperately want to run or fight, but you are frozen to the spot. You open your mouth to scream, but no sound comes out.

You have just experienced the fight-or-flight response. You took in data using your five senses, and your amygdala set off the alarm: "You are in danger!" Before your cortex even got the sensory info, and well before you could form a thought, your amygdala had already alerted your hypothalamus. And, in the first case, you were already primed to fight.

**. . . your rage beast hears the call and wants to brawl.**

Before you took that first punch, your hypothalamus got the signal and sent out chemical messages. Your neurons received those messages from their neighbors and released others. This triggered your adrenal glands, which began pumping adrenaline into your bloodstream. This caused your heart to beat faster, sending more blood to your muscles. You began to breathe faster, and you used more of your lungs so you could pull in more oxygen with every breath. All that oxygen hit your brain, sharpening your senses. Since you need a lot of energy to fight, your body put some processes (like digestion) on hold and began to load stored sugar and fat into your blood just in case you needed it.

Like a stretched rubber band, you were ready to snap into action. In a case like this, you have the options of running away or freezing, but your rage beast hears the call and wants to brawl.

# Prehistoric Cage Match

The fight-or-flight response is great for dealing with sudden threats to your safety. This was especially important for your prehistoric ancestors, whose likely threats had long, sharp fangs and powerful limbs. When you hear the phrase *stress response*, you might assume it means worry or fear, but anger—the fight part—was probably vital to helping your ancestors survive and advance.

If you imagine the first humans as burly fighters and fierce hunters, push that fantasy aside. Your earliest ancestors were more likely to be prey than predator. They probably passed their days collecting plants, scavenging carrion for leftovers, and avoiding animals that stalked them. But this doesn't mean they were running scared.

Prehistoric humans no doubt fought off terrifying predators when they needed to—saber-toothed tigers and cave bears, oh my. And even if most early humans were cooperative and peaceful, experts think they battled over territory sometimes.

Such survival threats are probably why humans began making and using tools, including weapons and fire. Remember, anger is being upset about something you see as doing you wrong—for example, a giant cat that wants to eat you on your doorstep. Or that you are always looking for berries when you could really go for a mammoth burger. Or the neighbors who want your cozy home for themselves. But anger isn't just feeling mad about those things in the moment. It's also the fire in your belly driving you to solve those problems.

For your ancient ancestors as cave-teens, stepping outside meant facing a world filled with threats to their survival. A system to alert them to danger and help them act quickly let them stay alive long enough to reproduce and pass on their genes. Fortunately for them (and you), that system also helped them become the ultimate predator.

# A Tale of Ancient Reactions

The urge to fight is an important part of your stress response—even if it is unlikely you will meet a ferocious predator on the way out your door. That drive to eliminate threats and conquer things has many other uses.

Scientists sometimes break the urge to fight—aggression—into categories that reveal the reasons behind it. Channeling anger to fight predators or enemies is *affective aggression*. This is a rage response for defending yourself. Sometimes the defensive stance isn't just about you. For instance, a mother, whether human or not, defending her babies against danger uses *maternal aggression*.

You probably also use *predatory aggression* to get the things you need or want. This is basically hunting, but it's not limited to stalking and killing your next meal. Have you ever wanted something so intensely that you could almost taste it? If the thing you want is something big and hard to get—like becoming a teen idol or running for class president—you might feel as if you were using your hunting drive to go after it. Such goal-seeking is called chasing your dreams for good reason!

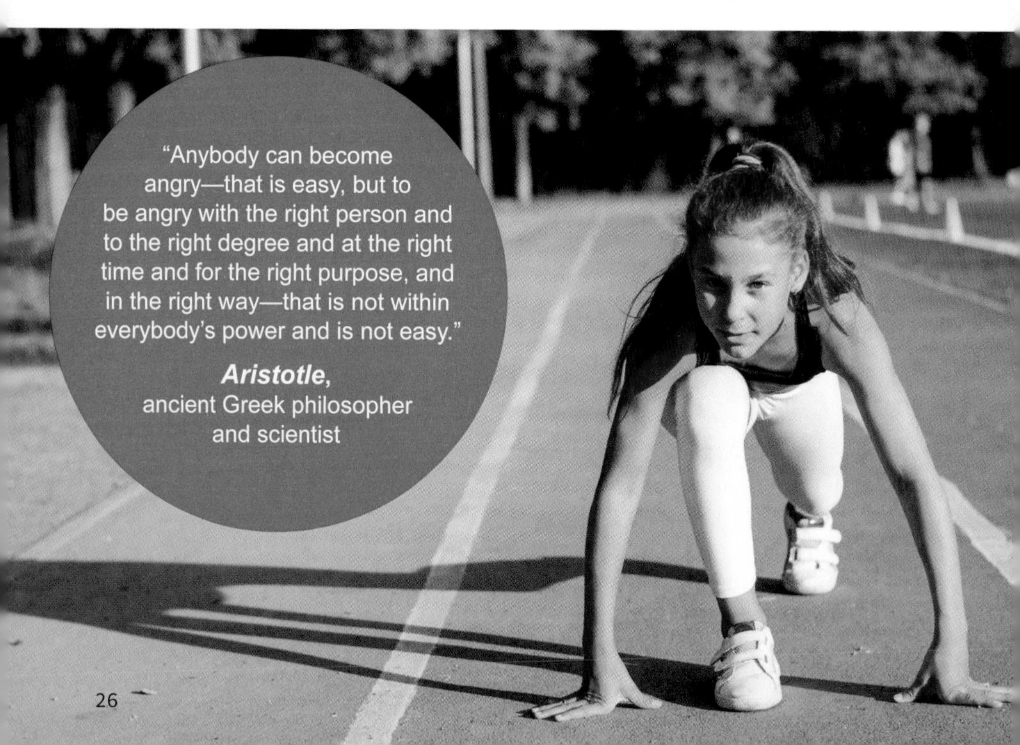

"Anybody can become angry—that is easy, but to be angry with the right person and to the right degree and at the right time and for the right purpose, and in the right way—that is not within everybody's power and is not easy."

***Aristotle***, ancient Greek philosopher and scientist

Humans sometimes use *within-species aggression* to decide who is in charge—a pecking order. Most people don't jump on their rivals and pluck them bald like actual chickens pecking for the chance to rule a literal roost. But there are lots of ways this drive shows up in people. Bullying may be a way of fighting for social power. You can even view sports or academics this way, since they're about fighting to win or come out on top.

These drives, just like your stress response, are passed down to you because they are a selective advantage—something that makes you better able to survive. They are there to help you succeed even when things get hard or obstacles show up.

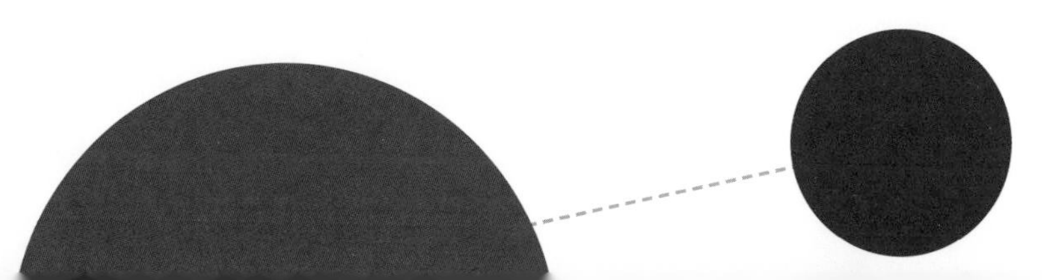

# ANGER AS A SOCIAL MOVER

Out-of-control anger can hurt you and those around you. However, when it comes to facing obstacles, well-controlled anger may be your best ally. The fire in your belly that urges you to fight for what you want or defend what you love has the power to change the world.

Kids' TV icon Mr. Rogers said to "look for the helpers" when viewing scary or sad news stories. Sometimes the helpers do obviously heroic things like digging through rubble for survivors. But some helpers work to tear down injustice. Whether those people shout on the floor of the Senate or silently protest at sports events, you can bet that the fire of anger drives social change.

That ribbon of motivating anger runs through every social movement in history. It was there when factory workers—including child laborers—stood up against unfair and dangerous working conditions. It was there when women faced imprisonment and abuse and still insisted on the right to vote. It was there in the civil rights movement, advocating for civil rights and racial justice. And it is still there when women of color point out that many of the women who fought for the right to vote also opposed voting rights for black men and pushed black women to the margins of the movement.

Anger can also be a privilege: something some people are allowed to do and others are not. An expert on the political power of anger points out that people with the most power are viewed as reasonable or patriotic when they get mad. People with less or very little power—such as women, people of color, disabled people, and poor people—can be called scary, unreasonable, or crazy when they express anger. Noticing who has the right to get mad is one way of identifying unfair treatment.

Feeling upset and channeling anger for good is a tricky but valuable skill. In fact, it's so easy to link anger with violence that a powerful form of activism recommends doing the opposite. Nonviolent protests, such as marches, sit-ins, strikes, and civil disobedience, bring attention and energy to social causes.

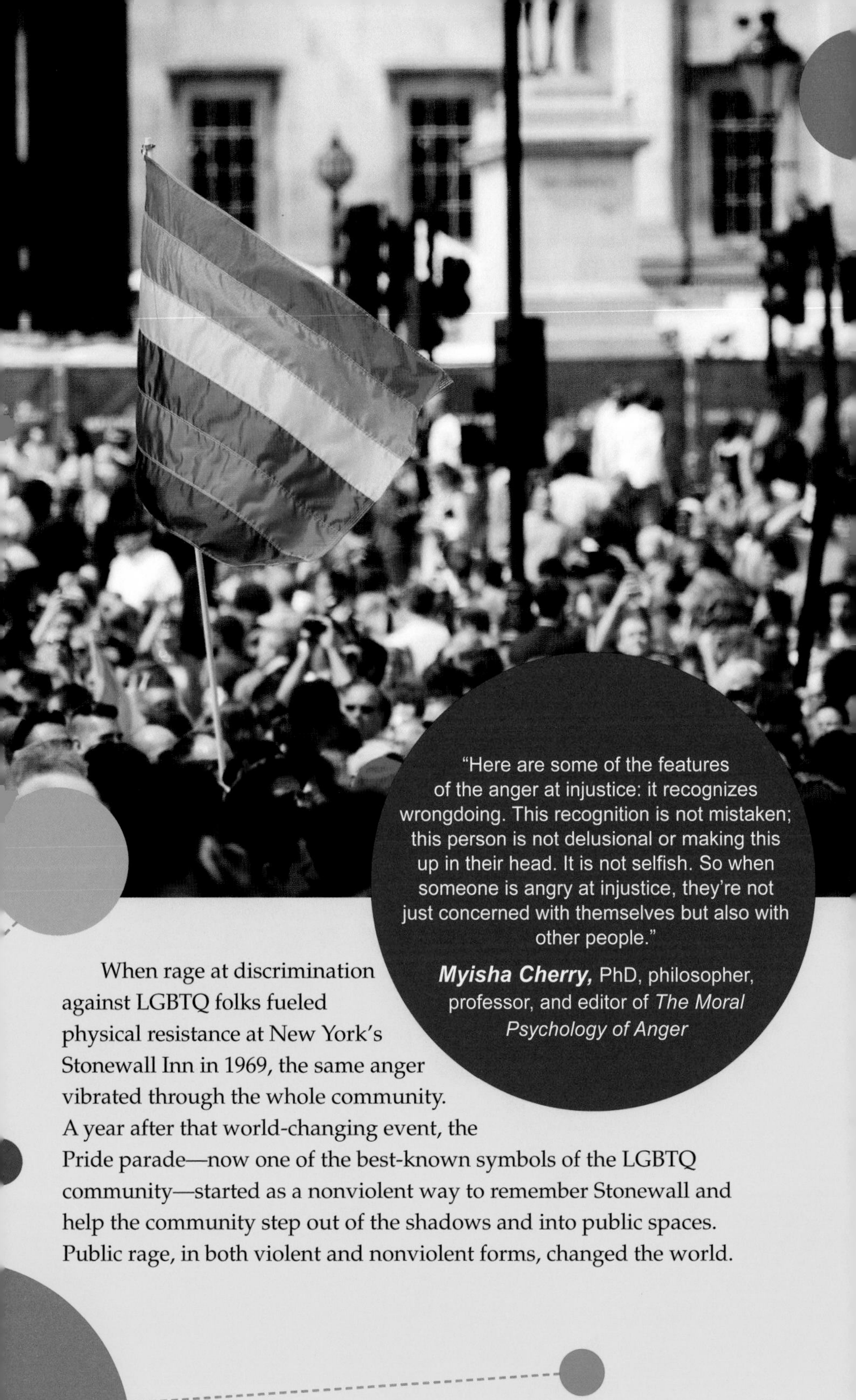

> "Here are some of the features of the anger at injustice: it recognizes wrongdoing. This recognition is not mistaken; this person is not delusional or making this up in their head. It is not selfish. So when someone is angry at injustice, they're not just concerned with themselves but also with other people."
>
> ***Myisha Cherry,*** PhD, philosopher, professor, and editor of *The Moral Psychology of Anger*

When rage at discrimination against LGBTQ folks fueled physical resistance at New York's Stonewall Inn in 1969, the same anger vibrated through the whole community. A year after that world-changing event, the Pride parade—now one of the best-known symbols of the LGBTQ community—started as a nonviolent way to remember Stonewall and help the community step out of the shadows and into public spaces. Public rage, in both violent and nonviolent forms, changed the world.

CHAPTER 4

# Rage Like a Boss

WHILE A WHITE-HOT RUSH of rage may happen before you think it through, figuring out how to deal with the anger takes a bit more effort. Your anger is there to make your life (and the world around you) better by pushing you to change things that aren't right. However, a quick temper can be distressing to you and others and even push people away. It takes work to find a balance.

# Know Your Anger

Few things spark rage as universally as the presence of an angry person right in front of you. Such an invasion of your personal space is a good gut-level definition of the word *violation*. Since anger signals a violation, figuring out why you feel violated can help you figure out how to deal with it.

Sometimes just knowing what causes your anger at the moment may be enough to let it go. You might be enraged when you see your journal moved from your drawer to the top of your dresser. If you suspect a parent rifled through your stuff and read your most private thoughts, your rage might grow—and you may need to figure out how to deal with what happened. But if you know your parent would never read your journal and simply moved it, you might just shrug off the violation of your space.

**Your anger is there to make your life (and the world around you) better . . .**

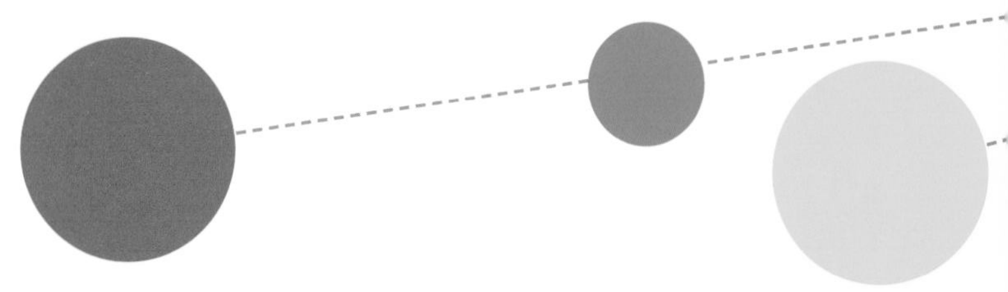

Remember the four needs common to most teens and young adults? You can use the acronym RSVP to remember them and check in when you feel a surge of anger.

## RESPECT

Did someone insult you, underestimate you, or make you feel small? Did the person ignore your boundaries?

## SPACE

Do you have all the physical and emotional room that you need, or is someone butting in?

## VALIDATION

Did someone make you feel as if your feelings weren't real or reasonable? Is someone refusing to hear you?

## PEERS

Do you feel that you don't fit in? Is someone keeping you from something you need to feel accepted?

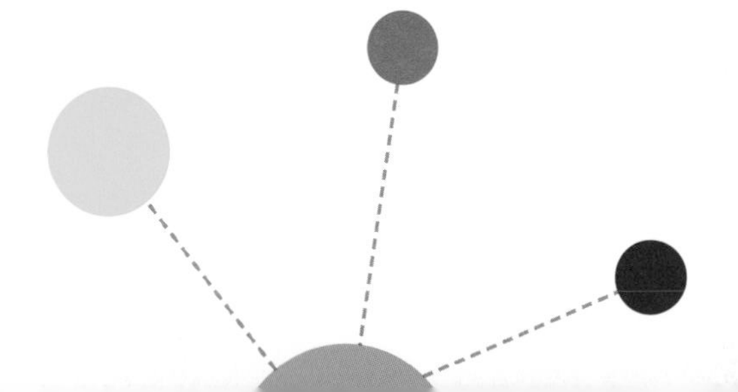

Neuroscientist R. Douglas Fields took an even deeper dive into what makes people snap. He listed nine universal causes of human anger. You can remember them with the acronym *LIFEMORTS*—the word doesn't make sense, but it still sticks in the brain.

- **LIFE OR DEATH:** Someone or something attacks you. If you don't fight, there is a good chance you will get hurt or die.
- **INSULT:** Someone does or says something in a rude or scornful way.
- **FAMILY:** Someone goes after the people you love or threatens to do so.
- **ENVIRONMENT:** Someone or something encroaches on your space or territory.
- **MATE:** Someone comes between you and your partner (or potential partner).
- **ORDER IN SOCIETY:** Someone or something is unjust or harmful to your community or the world.
- **RESOURCES:** Someone or something is stopping you from getting or keeping things you need or want.
- **TRIBE:** Someone or something threatens your group.
- **STOPPED:** Someone or something has you trapped or imprisoned.

## LIFEMORTS IRL

**Life or Death**
You are walking home when someone you don't know grabs you and tries to force you into a van.

**Insult**
Your frenemy finds your social media account and mocks your posts.

**Family**
You overhear someone saying something terrible about your mom.

**Environment**
You get home, and the door to your bedroom—which you keep closed—is standing wide open.

**Mate**
You see your BFF flirting with your crush.

**Order in Society**
Your principal insists it is OK for the dress code to target your gender unfairly.

**Tribe**
A member of an opposing sports team accuses your team of cheating.

**Resources**
Your parent says you can't have the game you want, even if you use your own money to buy it.

**Stopped**
Your friend is arguing with you, and every time you try to walk away, the friend blocks the door.

# First, the Terrible Ideas

Someone has trampled all over your needs or put a finger on one of your LIFEMORTS triggers. What do you do next? Some people see two options—swallow the anger or express it. Spoiler: Both have downsides.

You probably know that stuffing your anger down isn't going to end well. While lots of people do it anyway, the idea that swallowed anger damages the swallower is pretty widespread. Holding anger in (sometimes called repressing anger) can bring mental and physical suffering. It can even raise your risk of illnesses, such as heart disease.

So if you can't stuff it in, vent it out, right? Will screaming at the sky or beating a punching bag make it better? That'd be a no. Venting as a cure for anger is a myth. In fact, venting—also called *catharsis theory*—is also linked with an increased risk for illnesses, such as heart disease. What's more, it can come to feel like second nature, and that's not good for you or others. Research shows that venting makes you more likely to lash out with aggression, even at random people who have nothing to do with your rage. Venting throws gas on a fire.

"When you express your anger, you think that you are getting anger out of your system, but that's not true. When you express your anger, either verbally or with physical violence, you are feeding the seed of anger, and it becomes stronger in you."

***Thich Nhat Hanh,***
Buddhist monk, global spiritual leader, and peace activist

# Anger Scrubbers

In addition to venting or stuffing down your anger, there's a third option: remove the anger. This means working with your brain to reduce the amped-up state that comes with the surge of rage. Here are some tips for that.

**CHILL OUT:** Act like you're relaxed, even if you're not feeling it. Deep breathing and relaxing your muscles can cue your stress response to settle down. Other ideas include listening to calming music, doing quiet hobbies such as knitting or coloring, and trying mindfulness techniques like belly breathing.

## HOW TO BELLY BREATHE

Place one hand on your chest and one on your stomach near your belly button. Let out an annoyed sigh. (You can even say UGH.) With your mouth closed, slowly draw in air through your nose in a way that makes your stomach expand while your chest remains mostly still. Pause for a few seconds and then use your stomach muscles to slowly push the air out of your mouth. Repeat.

**GIVE YOURSELF TIME:** Some people say that surges of emotion only last about 90 seconds—unless you feed them. This is where the old-school advice to count to 100 before reacting comes in. If you can count your way through a surge of rage, you may be able to face the trigger with a cool head.

## HOW TO RELAX YOUR MUSCLES

Begin with an easy-to-isolate muscle group like your hands. Clench your fists as tightly as you can. Feel all the muscles in your hands and fingers and make them as tense as possible. Now release those muscles. Try to let your hands and fingers relax as much as possible. Do this for each set of muscles in your body. You can work from your feet to your face.

**SET A DATE WITH RAGE:**
Promise yourself that you will deal with what made you mad at a set time. Put it on your mental calendar and walk away. By the time your Rage Date rolls around, your stress response will be long gone and you can decide whether the cause still needs to be dealt with.

**REFRAME IT:** Is there another way to look at what's happening? This might work well if someone you care about (and who cares about you) triggered your rage. If you assume the best of them, what else could be going on? Is it possible they are just tired or crabby? Nobody wants you to be a doormat, but it's OK to let things slide sometimes.

**DISTRACT YOURSELF:** Do or think about something that makes you happy. Watch a movie. Play a game. Volunteer to help someone. Visit your friend's new puppy. Go for a walk outside. This stops you from turning the problem over and over in your mind.

## HOW TO FOREST BATHE

Borrow a Japanese wellness technique, shinrin-yoku or "forest bathing," and immerse yourself in nature. Step outside and away from technology for as long as you can. Wander around in a park or a forest. Use your senses to connect with the natural world. The benefits are mental relaxation and improved health. It's really hard to keep your fists clenched when you're hugging a tree.

# When Anger Is a Mask

Sometimes rage isn't the whole story. Anger can be a symptom of a whole slew of mental health conditions, including anxiety and depression. Some people present an angry face like a mask to hide more vulnerable feelings like sorrow, worry, or grief. It can be tough to peel back the mask and look at what's under it.

Anxiety and depression are more than just being too panicked or too worried or too sad. You can think of them as a reduced ability to regulate emotions. People with anxiety or depression also tend to have a negative bias in the way they process things. This makes them more prone to see things in a negative way and more tuned in to sadness and fear. When it teams up with rumination—turning something over and over in your mind—you can get stuck.

If you have a gut feeling that your anger is covering something else, reach out for help. Maybe you started feeling angry or moody after something bad happened, or you just feel stuck. Don't try to wait it out. These things do not mean you are crazy or broken or sick. There are people trained to help you get unstuck and feel better. You aren't alone.

**Sometimes rage isn't the whole story.**

# MINDFULNESS TRAINING

Your mind probably likes to wander off to other places and times. Maybe you obsess about things from the past or freak out about the future. Mindfulness is keeping your mind in the present moment.

Pretend that the present moment is like the earth, and you are a tree. Use your senses like roots digging into this moment and this place. Notice the sounds, smells, tastes, sights, and sensations around you right now. Carefully focus on the details you usually ignore. If your mind tries to run away, notice that too. It's OK. Just take notice and refocus.

Pick an easy task like coloring a picture. Turn off everything except your focus on that picture and the act of coloring it. Do you smell the crayon wax? Hear it scraping against the paper? Do you feel the soft paper in your hand? See the way the bits of wax pull off the crayon and cling to the paper? This focus on the present is an example of mindfulness.

You can be mindful of your anger too. This means noticing all the things happening inside your mind and your body without judging them or trying to stop. Simply notice that the rage exists and how it feels.

CHAPTER 5

# How Angry Is Too Angry?

LEARNING THE INS AND OUTS OF ANGER is great, but what if you feel like you can't control your anger? At some point, you might wonder whether you (or a friend) have an anger problem. If anger seems to be masking something else—such as anxiety or depression—it might be time to think about getting help with those things too.

Your anger might become a problem if you have these red flags:

- **It comes on fast and strong.** Do you feel irritable or on edge basically all the time? Do small frustrations spark a big rage reaction?
- **It includes violence.** Do you hit things or people or break things when you are angry, or daydream about doing so? Do you yell and scream at people or say hurtful things?
- **It comes with uncomfortable physical symptoms.** Do you feel a tingling or get headaches, a racing heart or tight chest, pressure in your head or sinuses, or exhaustion along with your rage?
- **It cycles with remorse.** Do you feel very sorry right after an angry outburst? Do you notice a pattern of raging and then trying to make up for hurting people or damaging things while you were angry?
- **It comes with maladaptive behaviors.** People sometimes use these harmful actions to try to deal with uncomfortable feelings. Some are minor, like biting your fingernails or picking at your skin. But major maladaptive behaviors are a sign that you should reach out for help. These include disordered eating or exercising (such as not eating enough or eating too much, throwing up after eating, or exercising more than is healthy) and self-harm, which is cutting, burning, or otherwise hurting yourself to release emotional pain.

Rage is also strongly linked with substance abuse, especially among teens and young adults. Out-of-control anger increases your risk of using drugs and alcohol, and using drugs and alcohol makes anger worse. Young people with high levels of anger who use drugs and alcohol are more likely to have problems with the law. They also need more help to address addiction. While everyone should be careful about deciding whether to use drugs and alcohol, this is especially true if you have a hard time managing your anger.

If you notice any red flags in your anger, ask for help. Anger can become a problem, but it doesn't have to stay that way, and you don't have to face it alone. Lots of people need support to manage anger. You deserve to feel in charge of your life and your feelings.

# Anger Disorder Symptoms

Everyone feels angry sometimes. When you're going through a tough time, it can be hard to get your anger under control until the stress lessens. However, when rage rears up easily and often over a long period of time, it might be part of an anger disorder. Here is a list of how anger can appear as a symptom of the anger disorders.

**PEOPLE WITH ANXIETY DISORDERS:**

- Have a hard time concentrating and sleeping.
- Sometimes have racing or disturbing thoughts.
- May feel always on alert.
- May feel irritable or have bursts of anger.
- Have excessive worry or panic attacks.

**PEOPLE WITH DEPRESSION:**

- Lose interest in things they once liked.
- Have a hard time concentrating or feel bogged down.
- May feel agitated or irritable.
- May lash out or snap at loved ones.
- Sometimes have trouble sleeping or want to sleep all the time.

**PEOPLE WITH PTSD:**

- Have symptoms of anxiety or depression after a terrifying experience.
- Have nightmares or flashbacks of what happened.
- May feel that they are in fight-or-flight mode all the time.

**PEOPLE WITH INTERMITTENT EXPLOSIVE DISORDER:**

- Have sudden bursts of rage that seem to come out of nowhere.
- May scream, throw things, damage things, or get physical during outbursts.
- May have physical symptoms before or during an outburst, such as racing thoughts, tingling, or shaking.

**PEOPLE WITH DISRUPTIVE BEHAVIOR DISORDERS SUCH AS OPPOSITIONAL DEFIANT DISORDER (ODD) AND CONDUCT DISORDER:**

- May have bursts of rage or tantrums.
- Often have a hard time with authority figures and following rules.
- May annoy others on purpose or bully them.
- Sometimes have problems with the law.
- May hurt other people or animals.

**PEOPLE WITH ADJUSTMENT DISORDER WITH DISTURBANCE OF CONDUCT:**

- Have a hard time handling a change or a specific stressor.
- May have bursts of rage.
- May have big mood swings and act out because of them.
- May do things to get revenge or hurt other people.

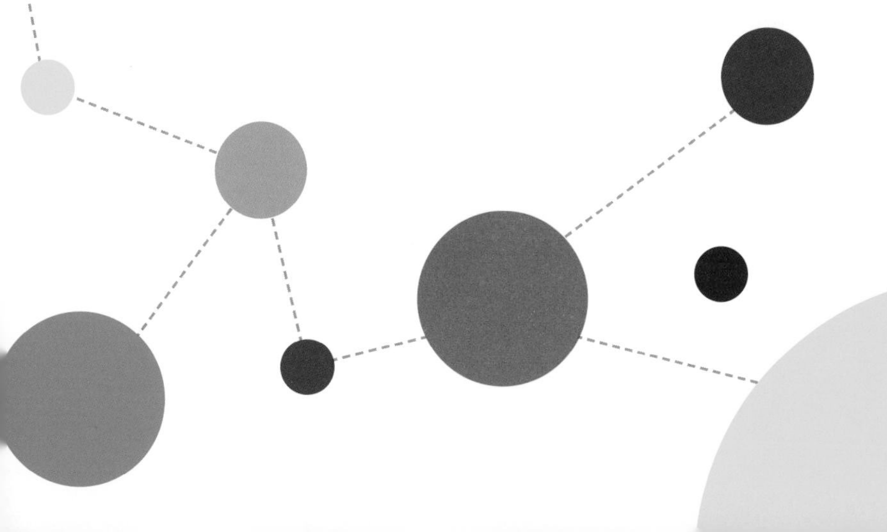

# How to Get Help

If you think your anger might be a problem, it is important to ask for help. Anger and anger disorders are treatable. This means you can feel better! The best thing you can do is get help from someone trained to treat anger. Only a mental health professional can diagnose and treat a mental health disorder.

Mental health professionals can be therapists, clinical social workers, counselors, psychologists, or psychiatrists. They have specific training to diagnose and treat mental health concerns. They should be licensed by your state. Choosing a licensed professional means you can trust that they will follow the rules and use therapy methods that are backed up by science.

Many therapists list the types of problems they usually treat, so you can look for someone who is an expert in anger. Find an adult you trust to help you. If you know that something else might come up during therapy (for example, LGBTQ identity or substance abuse), it is a good idea to make sure the therapist can deal with those things too. Since you may be sharing private or sensitive information with your therapist, you want to pick someone you like and who shares your values.

If you or your parents or guardians aren't sure where to start, some places to ask for a referral include:

- Your school counselor
- Your doctor
- Your health insurance company
- A local hospital or medical clinic, such as Planned Parenthood
- A local college or university
- A professional database, such as the Anxiety and Depression Association of America's list at www.adaa.org

If you suspect your anger comes from a painful experience, look for a therapist or counselor with training in trauma-informed care. This type of treatment focuses on using your personal strengths to help you feel safe and in control.

Reaching out for support isn't always easy, and some people face extra barriers. For instance, some people have cultural beliefs about mental health that make it harder to ask for support. People of color have the same rates of mental health disorders that white people do, but they are much less likely to seek treatment. Organizations like the Boris Lawrence Henson Foundation and the Steve Fund hope to change this. They are working to end stigmas attached to mental illness and health care among people of color, and they are trying to increase cultural awareness and sensitivity among therapists. The Steve Fund offers scholarships for researchers studying the mental health needs of students of color and for students of color entering the field of mental health care.

For some people, money is a barrier to therapy. Free or low-cost options include finding a counselor who accepts payments from your insurer, a counselor who uses a sliding scale, or a donation-based support group run by professional therapists at a local community center.

Privacy concerns may also make it hard for kids under the age of 18 to get help. Young people who are LGBTQ and live with unsupportive families may worry about being outed by a therapist or undergoing therapy that doesn't affirm their identities. Teens who use drugs or alcohol may be afraid of being punished or worry about disappointing people they love. Check your state laws about getting therapy as a minor for more information.

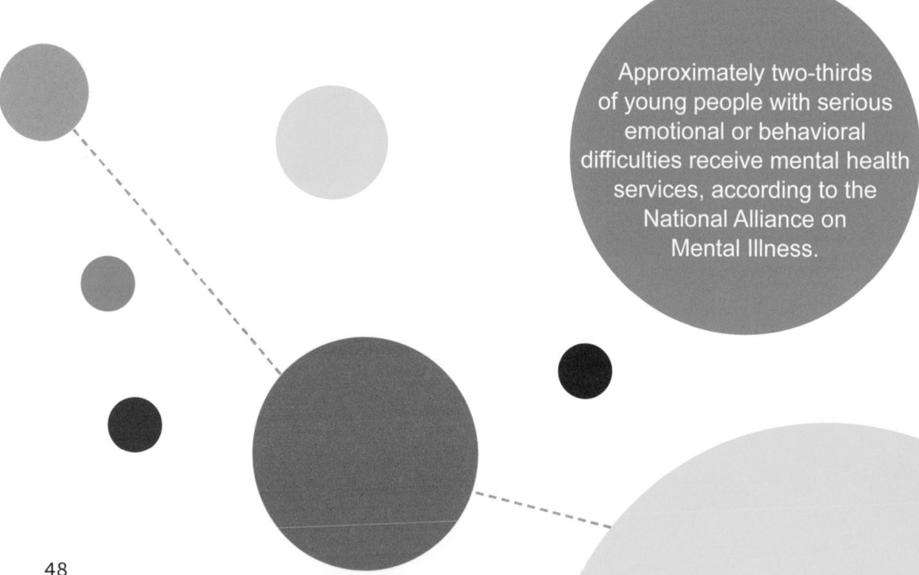

## WHAT HAPPENS IN THERAPY?

When you picture counseling, do you imagine lying on a couch while a bearded guy stiffly asks, "And how does that make you *feel*?"

It's not usually like that. Visiting a therapist can feel weird, especially if you are private about your feelings. Sometimes people worry that seeing a therapist means they are crazy or mentally ill. This isn't true! A therapist is just someone who has tools to help you look at your feelings and thought processes in new ways.

An important thing to know about therapy is that you have the right to expect confidentiality about most things. However, if you are under the age of 18, it is important to ask therapists what, if anything, they would need to tell your parents. This is because the law is unclear when it comes to disclosing information about minors, and you should know what to expect before you begin therapy.

The first session with a new therapist is likely to seem a bit like a job interview. You might hire this person to help you solve personal problems, so take the time to ask questions and get a feel for how the therapist responds. At a first meeting, therapists will usually tell you about themselves, their training, and types of treatment offered in their practice. Some therapists will explain that they assign homework between sessions (such as practicing skills you learn).

Once you begin seeing a therapist, you can expect to bring up a topic yourself or have the therapist suggest one. The therapist will probably take notes to help prepare for the next visit. Some people attend therapy only a few times, while others go regularly for months or years at a time.

CHAPTER 6

# You Are in Control

EVEN HEALTHY ANGER can feel overwhelming sometimes. The good news is this: You have the tools to manage it. When rage threatens to take over, your brain already has ways of taming the rampaging Hulk.

## Brain Putty

Since the time you were born, your brain hasn't stopped changing. The brain is more like moldable putty than a firm, unyielding rock. Scientists call this *brain plasticity*. The idea is that your brain is flexible and capable of responding to psychological pressure, just as soft plastic bends under physical pressure.

Even the number of neurons in your brain keeps changing. Scientists have discovered that your hippocampus and the smell-associated areas of your brain add about 700 new neurons every single day. They lose even more. This turnover of nerve cells is important for plasticity and neural adaptability and likely affects learning, memory, and (drumroll) emotional regulation, which includes anger control.

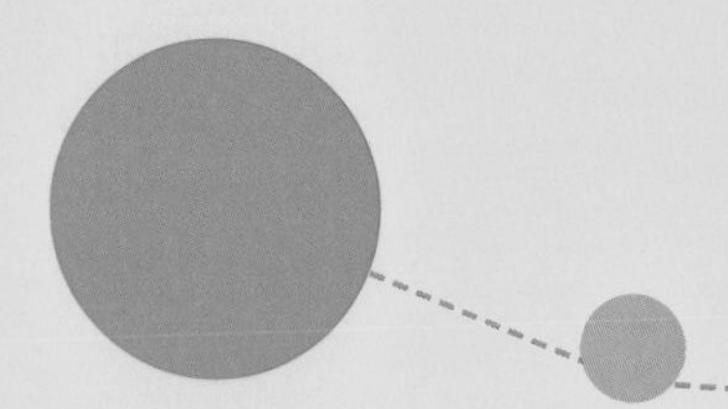

Your synapses also change a lot over time. If you could go back in time and peek into your toddler brain, you would see around 15,000 synapses per neuron at age 2. That means each of your nerve cells had 15,000 places to make connections with its neighbors. Between that time and your early 20s, you lose about half of those synapses through a process called *synaptic pruning*. If that term makes you imagine your brain as a plant that needs trimming into shape, hold onto your hat—because it gets weirder.

Inside your brain, microglial cells remove damage or infection by phagocytosis, which means "to devour." These cells basically travel through your brain and eat things that are problems.

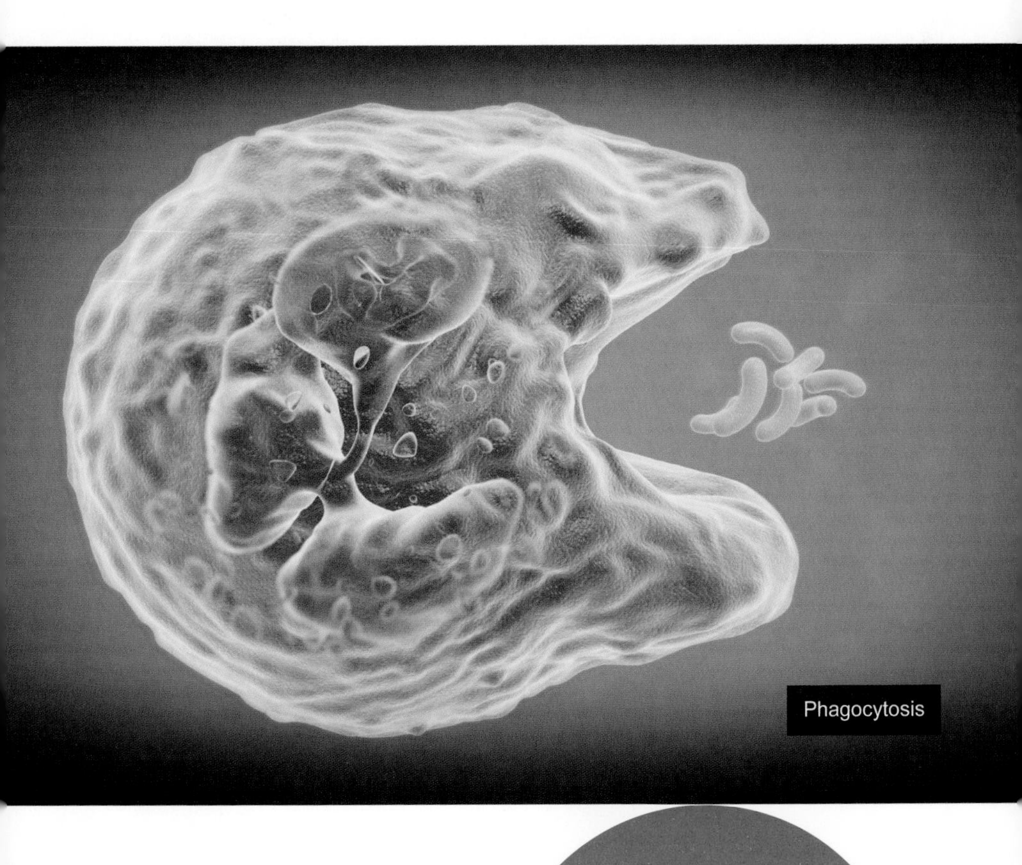
Phagocytosis

# Winner, Winner, Chicken Dinner

While you can't literally unhinge your skull and squish your plastic brain around like dough, you can use your brain's adaptable nature to your benefit. Brain plasticity is closely related to resilience. This is your ability to adapt to stressors and bounce back when things are hard. Your brain changes as part of its normal development. It also changes when things get tough.

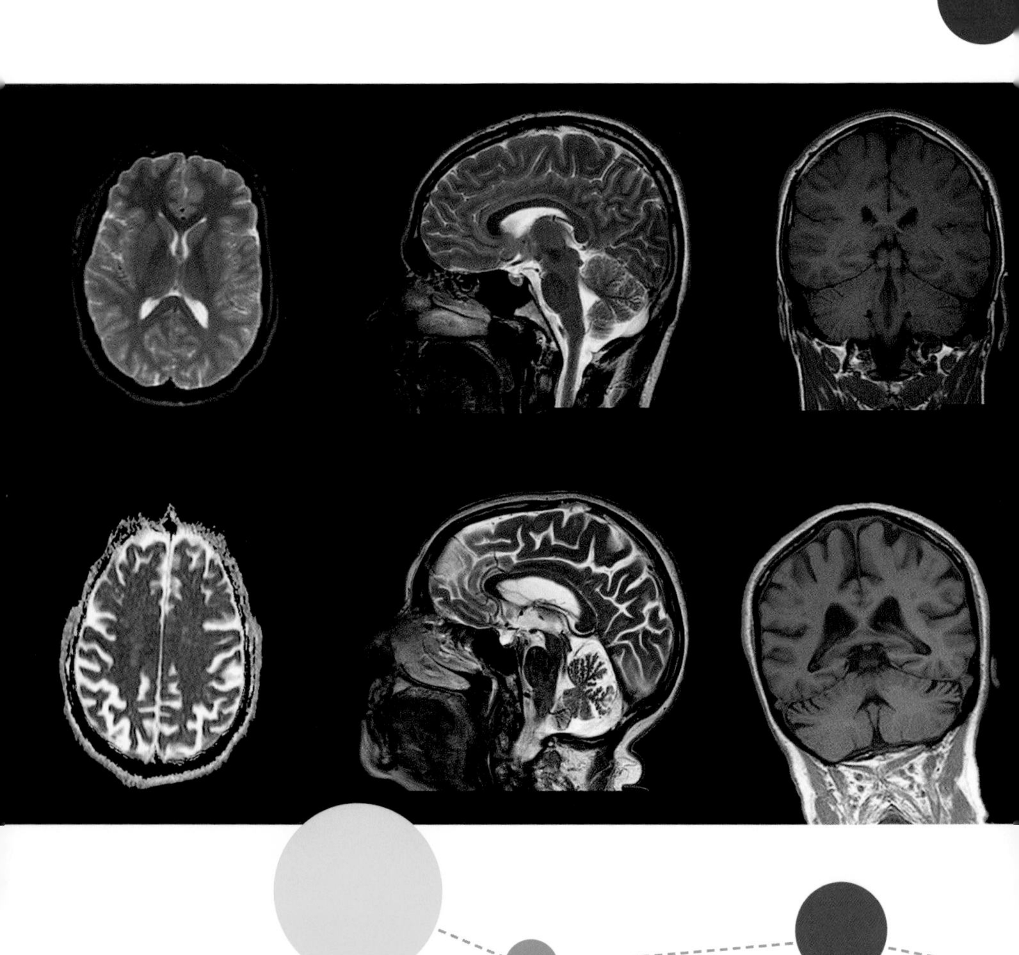

# Brain plasticity is closely related to resilience.

Some of these changes aren't so great. Stress and trauma can shrink your hippocampus and prefrontal cortex, as well as the branchy arms of your nerve cells. Given what you know about how important these areas are for emotional regulation, that probably doesn't sound awesome. But there's good news. Positive things can change the brain in the opposite way, enlarging those areas that stress shrinks. Brain boosters include exercise, learning new things, social support, and mindfulness exercises. Some scientists say these behaviors open windows of plasticity. These and other healthy activities seem to give your brain the chance to bounce back from stress—and make you more resilient in the face of adversity.

Anger isn't just a base human instinct that evolution held onto for no reason. It is a powerful tool that alerts you when something is wrong and gives you the drive to fix it. Your early human ancestors probably used anger to fight off predators snarling outside their caves and to perform impressive feats in the face of calamity. It also probably helped them to organize their families and communities and to take action when they needed to change leaders or revamp whole social structures.

If your oldest ancestors could harness strong emotions like that, just imagine what you can do. You are living at the safest time ever in human history. You have knowledge and tools that would have blown your Stone Age ancestors' minds. And you still carry remnants of their DNA in yours. Their drive to survive and thrive? That is your legacy. That incredible resilience is like a spark passed from the first human in your line all the way to you, where you keep it alive in every single cell of your body. Putting your own story into context might just make you stronger.

# Methods for Cultivating Resilience

You probably already know many of the things you can do to increase your resilience. Take a look at the American Psychological Association's list of resilience builders.

## APA Ways to Build Resilience

Take decisive actions

Keep things in perspective

Avoid seeing crises as insurmountable problems

Move toward your goals

Maintain a hopeful outlook

Nurture a positive view of yourself

Positive choices you make every day buffer the risks of stress. This means eating healthy foods, exercising, and getting 9 to 11 hours of good sleep every night.

Another way to build resilience is forming strong support networks of friends and family. It doesn't really matter if your people are found online or in real life—or if your family is by blood, adoption, or choice. Having just one person you can count on, no matter what, can make all the difference in your ability to bounce back from hard times. Don't worry if you don't have that one person in your life right now. Your built-in resilience is there for you, and it can help you reach out and find others who will appreciate you.

Look for opportunities for self-discovery

Take care of yourself

Accept that change is a part of living

If resilience were an Olympic sport (or a post-apocalyptic survival scenario in which roving humans trade bottle caps for rat steaks), two activities that can help you stay competitive are mindfulness training and play.

Mindfulness—learning to stay in the present and not be distracted by past and future dramas that play out in your head—keeps you sharp. It gives you perspective and builds your stamina for managing strong emotions like anger. You already know that if you can figure out what a burst of anger signals, you can channel the power of that emotion.

Play is an underrated human activity. It is the way humans make sense of the world, learn new things, and let off steam. Imagine a pair of lion cubs wrestling and play fighting. Is their play silly, or are they practicing skills they will need later? The things you do for fun aren't silly, either. In fact, experts point out that young people need big stretches of time to play and figure out life on their own terms.

# Use Your Voice

Building community and support networks for yourself makes a big difference. It's also important to look honestly at how you fit into the world around you, and to help provide that community and support for other people.

Remember what Mr. Rogers said about looking for the helpers? That's an awesome tool for helping really little kids see terrible things without feeling scared. Once you're no longer tiny, it isn't enough to just *look* for the helpers. You *are* the helpers. When you see or experience something that makes you mad because it feels wrong or unjust, you have the right to speak your mind. Even if you think nobody will listen or your voice is too quiet.

There are probably ways in which you are lucky and ways in which you need to work harder than other people. You are wise enough to know that the world isn't as just as it could be. Some people are born with advantages based on things they can't control—like skin color, sex, or gender identity. When it comes to anger, even expressing strong emotions can be a privilege. Some people seem to be allowed to be as angry as they want to be while other people are told to calm down or are even punished for getting mad.

In the places where you have more of a voice, you can do something even more powerful than speaking up. You can use your voice to make the voices of other people louder. This is especially useful if you are angry about an injustice that doesn't affect you personally. Look for expert voices speaking up about those issues and use yours to boost the message.

**You can use your voice to make the voices of other people louder.**

"We've all got both light and dark inside us. What matters is the part we choose to act on. That's who we really are."

***Sirius Black,***
*Harry Potter and the Order of the Phoenix* (film)

## STUDENT ACTIVISM

In 2018 the deadliest high school shooting to take place so far thrust a group of student survivors into the spotlight. Among them was Emma Gonzalez, a high school senior who brought nonviolent activism to the stage. At the March for Our Lives protest, Gonzalez stood silent at the mic for more than six minutes—the amount of time the victims had endured the shooting. Those long moments gave people the chance to sit with uncomfortable feelings and grief—and it was called the most powerful part of the protest.

In the months that followed, teens like Gonzalez stepped up and revealed their pain—or stood silent and showed their pain in ways nobody could ignore. They refused to stuff their pain and anger down out of sight. These kids were enraged that the adults around them had failed to protect them—especially their elected officials, who were still trying to ignore a gun-control crisis that had been building for almost 20 years.

About her activism and hopes for the future, Gonzalez said it "is probably gonna be years, and at this point, I don't know that I mind. Nothing that's worth it is easy. . . . We could very well die trying to do this. But we could very well die *not* trying to do this, too. So why not die for something rather than nothing?"

Whether you are working to solve problems in society or chasing your dreams, you can count on your anger to alert you when something is wrong. If you learn to control that fire and use it to shine a light for other people to see, you can be the change the world needs.

# Reach Out

Text with a trained crisis counselor 24/7 by texting HOME to 741741. Students of color can also text STEVE to 741741 for crisis counseling designed for communities of color through a partnership between CTL and the Steve Fund.

*Crisis Text Line:*
www.crisistextline.org

Check out resources for supporting the mental and emotional health of students of color.

*The Steve Fund:*
https://www.stevefund.org/

Find support for mental health issues in the African American community.

*The Boris Lawrence Henson Foundation:*
https://borislhensonfoundation.org/

Talk with crisis counselors from the LGBTQ community via Trevor Project and Trans Lifeline.

*Trevor Project:*
www.thetrevorproject.org

*Trans Lifeline:*
www.translifeline.org

Find a safe space to share your feelings and read others' stories at this website sponsored by the National Alliance on Mental Illness (NAMI).

*Ok2Talk:*
ok2talk.org

Find a therapist or support group.

*Anxiety and Depression Association of America:*
adaa.org/netforum/findatherapist

# Glossary

**aggression**—behavior meant to harm or control someone

**carrion**—meat left over after one animal is killed and eaten by another animal

**catharsis theory**—the idea that negative feelings can be released or processed through sudden, intense displays of emotion

**civil disobedience**—refusal to obey governmental commands, especially as a nonviolent way of forcing certain action by the government

**confidentiality**—rules or promises to keep something private

**disordered eating or exercising**—closely controlling how much you eat or exercise. This includes behaviors such as not eating enough, making yourself throw up after eating, and exercising too much.

**emotional regulation**—feeling all your emotions but holding back some reactions when you need to

**maladaptive behaviors**—harmful things people may do to ease uncomfortable feelings

**microglial cells**—support cells in your brain that remove damage or infection and trim your synapses

**mindfulness**—staying present; noticing your feelings and thoughts without judging them

**negative bias**—tendency to notice painful or bad things

**phagocytosis**—process by which a cell changes shape to surround and destroy something (like bacteria)

**plasticity**—ability to change or be molded

**privilege**—advantage not available to everyone

**resilience**—ability to bounce back from hard times

**rumination**—thinking about something over and over

**selective advantage**—characteristic that makes you better able to survive in your environment

**self-harm**—causing pain or damage to your own body by cutting, burning, or scratching the skin to release emotional pain.

**trauma-informed care**—treatment for survivors of painful experiences that focuses on using their strengths to help them feel safe and in control

**trigger**—something that activates difficult emotions or reminds you of a trauma

**violation**—something that makes you feel disrespected or disregards your rights

# Additional Resources

## Further Reading

Daniels, Natasha. *Anxiety Sucks! A Teen Survival Guide.* Scotts Valley, CA: CreateSpace, 2016.

Lee, Chanice. *Young Revolutionary: A Teen's Guide to Activism.* Atlanta, GA: Literary Revolutionary, 2018.

Purcell, Mark C. *Mindfulness for Teen Anger.* Oakland, CA: New Harbinger Publications, 2014.

Saltzman, Amy. *A Still Quiet Place for Teens: A Mindfulness Workbook to Ease Stress and Difficult Emotions.* Oakland, CA: New Harbinger Publications, 2016.

## Internet Sites

*American Psychological Association*
www.apa.org

*GLSEN—Gay/Straight Student Alliances*
www.glsen.org

*National Alliance on Mental Illness*
www.nami.org

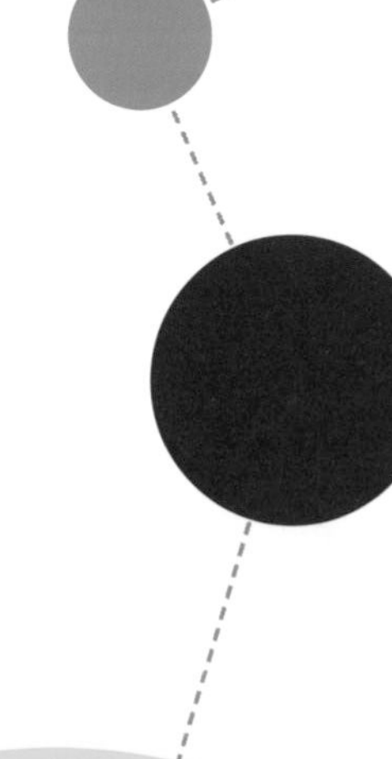

# Critical Thinking Questions

## 1

Scientists who study angry outbursts noted an increase in the number of expressions of anger among adolescents (compared with younger children or adults). What factors do you think increase anger during this life stage? How do you think adults could better support young people during this time?

## 2

Some experts say that expressing anger is a privilege. Give an example from real life of: 1) someone who is considered powerful or passionate for expressing anger, and 2) someone who is considered threatening or irrational for expressing anger. (Hint: Think about historical figures and celebrities.) Why do you think the examples you chose are viewed differently for showing anger?

## 3

Some people seem more resilient than others. List all the factors you can think of that might make someone better able to handle hard times. Use the text and your own thinking skills.

# Source Notes

p. 7, "a belief that we . . ." Farzaneh Pahlavan, ed. *Multiple Facets of Anger.* New York: Nova Science, 2010, p. i.

p. 19, "Cells that fire . . ." Carla J. Shatz, "The Developing Brain," *Scientific American* 267, no. 3, Special Issue: Mind and Brain, September 1992, p. 64.

p. 21, "With great power . . ." Stan Lee, "Introducing Spider Man," *Amazing Fantasy* 1, no. 15, August 10, 1962, p. 12.

p. 29, "Here are some of the features . . ." Rebecca Traister. *Good and Mad.* New York: Simon & Schuster, 2018, p. xxiii.

p. 36, "When you express . . ." John Malkin, interview with Thich Nhat Hanh, "In Engaged Buddhism, Peace Begins with You," *Lion's Roar,* July 1, 2003, https://www.lionsroar.com/in-engaged-buddhism-peace-begins-with-you/ Accessed April 9, 2019.

p. 56, "We've all got both light and dark . . ." *Harry Potter and the Order of the Phoenix,* directed by David Yates, 2007, London: Heyday Films, DVD.

p. 57, "is probably gonna be years. . ." Joan Walsh, "6 Minutes and 20 Seconds That Could Change the World," *Salon,* March 24, 2018, https://www.thenation.com/article/6-minutes-and-20-seconds-that-could-change-the-world/ Accessed April 9, 2019.

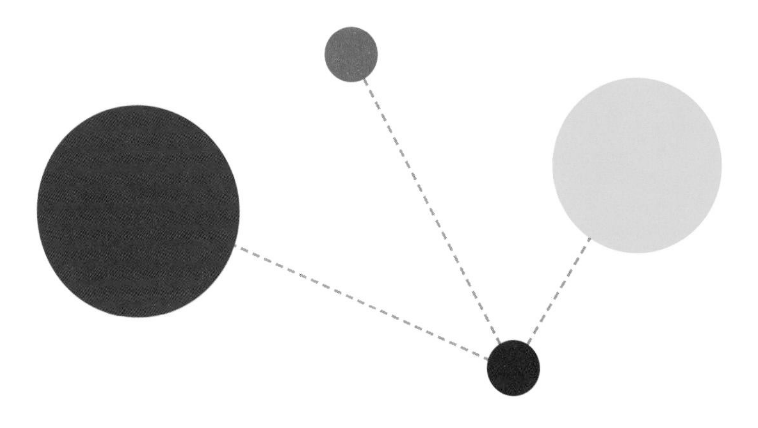

# Select Bibliography


Abblett, Mitch R. *Helping Your Angry Teen*. Oakland, CA: New Harbinger Publications, 2017.

American Psychological Association, "The Road to Resilience," https://www.apa.org/helpcenter/road-resilience.aspx Accessed January 20, 2019.

Anxiety and Depression Association of America, "Anxiety and Depression," https://adaa.org/sites/default/files/Anxiety%20and%20Depression.pdf Accessed January 20, 2019.

Bradley, Michael J. *Crazy-Stressed*. New York: AMACOM, 2017.

Bushman, Brad, "Anger Management: What Works and What Doesn't," *Psychology Today*, September 25, 2013, https://www.psychologytoday.com/us/blog/get-psyched/201309/anger-management-what-works-and-what-doesnt Accessed April 9, 2019.

Chemaly, Soraya L. *Rage Becomes Her*. New York: Atria Books, 2018.

Diamond, Stephen, "Anger Disorder: What It Is and What We Can Do About It," *Psychology Today*, April 3, 2009, https://www.psychologytoday.com/us/blog/evil-deeds/200904/anger-disorder-what-it-is-and-what-we-can-do-about-it Accessed April 16, 2019.

Fields, R. Douglas. *Why We Snap: Understanding the Rage Circuit in Your Brain*. New York: Dutton, 2016.

Greenberg, Melanie. *The Stress-Proof Brain*. Oakland, CA: New Harbinger Publications, 2017.

Grohol, John, "Why So Angry and Irritable? It Might Be Depression," PsychCentral, July 8, 2018, https://psychcentral.com/blog/why-so-angry-irritable-it-might-be-depression/ Accessed April 9, 2019.

Harvard Health Publishing, "Understanding the Stress Response," Harvard Medical School, May 1, 2018, https://www.health.harvard.edu/staying-healthy/understanding-the-stress-response Accessed April 9, 2019.

Jones, Lindsey, et al., "Use of Selected Nonmedication Mental Health Services by Adolescent Boys and Girls with Serious Emotional or Behavioral Difficulties: United States, 2010–2012," National Center for Health Statistics Data Brief No. 163, August 2014, https://www.cdc.gov/nchs/products/databriefs/db163.htm Accessed April 16, 2019.

Lee, Stan, "Introducing Spider Man," *Amazing Fantasy* 1, no. 15, August 10, 1962.

National Institute for the Clinical Application of Behavioral Medicine, "How Anger Affects the Brain and Body [infographic]," 2017, https://www.nicabm.com/how-anger-affects-the-brain-and-body-infographic/ Accessed April 9, 2019.

O'Neil, Dennis, "Early Human Culture," *Early Human Evolution*, 2014, https://www2.palomar.edu/anthro/homo/homo_4.htm Accessed April 9, 2019.

Pahlavan, Farzaneh, ed. *Multiple Facets of Anger*. New York: Nova Science, 2010.

Pittman, Catherine M., and Elizabeth M. Karle. *Rewire Your Anxious Brain*. Oakland, CA: New Harbinger Publications, 2015.

Potegal, Michael, et al., eds., "A Brief History of Anger," *International Handbook of Anger*, pp. 9–24. New York: Springer, 2010. https://www.researchgate.net/publication/226179869_A_Brief_History_of_Anger Accessed April 9, 2019.

Powledge, Tabitha, "Do the MAOA and CDH13 'Human Warrior Genes' Make Violent Criminals—and What Should Society Do?" *Genetic Literacy Project*, July 29, 2016, https://geneticliteracyproject.org/2016/07/29/does-the-human-warrior-gene-make-violent-criminals-and-what-should-society-do/# Accessed April 9, 2019.

Primm, Annelle B., "College Students of Color: Overcoming Mental Health Challenges," *NAMI Blog*, July 16, 2018, https://nami.org/Blogs/NAMI-Blog/July-2018/College-Students-of-Color-Overcoming-Mental-Healt Accessed April 9, 2019.

Saltz, Gail. *The Power of Different*. New York: Flatiron Books, 2017.

Carla J. Shatz, "The Developing Brain," *Scientific American*, 267, no. 3, Special Issue: Mind and Brain, September 1992, pp. 60–67.

Traister, Rebecca. *Good and Mad*. New York: Simon & Schuster, 2018.

Worrall, Simon, "Your Brain is Hardwired to Snap," *National Geographic*, February 7, 2016, https://news.nationalgeographic.com/2016/02/160207-brain-violence-rage-snap-science-booktalk/ Accessed April 9, 2019.

# Index



# About the Author

Melissa Mayer is a science writer and former science teacher who lives in Portland, Oregon, with her wife, kids, and way too many animals—dogs, cats, rabbits, and chickens. She's super nerdy and loves writing and talking about molecular biology and protein folding. She is a trained crisis counselor who loves bonfires and hot springs.